Praise for Ethics in a Nutshell

is a terrific short survey book —engaging, accessible, and wonderfully succinct.

I recommend it for the beginning of applied ethics courses with high interdisciplinary enrollment (environmental ethics, business ethics, animal ethics, bioethics, etc.) in order to bring students with no philosophical background quickly up to speed in the basic methodology of the field, or even at the beginning of an ethical theory course as a way to preview what's to come."

- Philosophy Professor Jennifer Everett, Co-Director of Environmental Fellows Program, DePauw University, Indiana

"Informative, concise, and entertaining! Deaton's ethics primer is the best short introduction to ethics out there and covers the basics of ethical theory in a careful and lively manner. The book deftly navigates highly controversial issues in a way that is sensitive to opposing points of view.

It is perfect for an intro-level philosophy class, but I have also used it successfully in the first couple weeks of an upper-level ethics class. I would recommend it to anyone who wants to teach or learn the gist of philosophical ethics as quickly as possible."

- Assistant Professor of Philosophy and Religion Greg Bock, Director of UT Tyler Center for Ethics, AAR Western Region Ethics Co-Chair, University of Texas at Tyler

"Deaton's passion and clarity for teaching ethics is exemplified in *Ethics in a Nutshell.* In addition to covering the most prominent moral theories, he illustrates how philosophical ethics differs from religion and politics, the problems of moral relativism, important features of moral language, and common argumentative techniques. Deaton makes understanding ethics engaging and fun.

I've used it in many of my own ethics courses, and have never been disappointed. Teachers, students, and anyone seeking to gain a secure grasp of ethics should read this book."

- Assistant Professor and Program Coordinator of Philosophy and Religious Studies Court Lewis, Owensboro Community and Technical College, Kentucky

Supplement *Ethics in a Nutshell* with an "Ask Matt" interface, sample reflection questions and video lectures at

EthicsinaNutshell.org

"Ethics in a Nutshell combined with Professor Matt's YouTube lecture videos made philosophical ethics engaging and easy to understand.

I highly recommend it not only to students majoring in philosophy, but to those simply willing to push the boundaries of their views."

- Criminal Justice Undergraduate Gabriel Gray, University of Texas at Tyler

Ask Matt

Andrew T   7/5/2017 08:31:27 pm

If I'm a logger and I cut down the oldest tree in the world (which happens to be on my property), is that inherently unethical?
What if that tree contained the only cure for a horrible disease, but I didn't know?

Reply

Matt →   7/7/2017 03:02:45 pm

Hey Andrew,

Thanks so much for your question.

I should admit up front that environmental ethics is not my area of specialization. I've dabbled in it, but am more competent in bioethics and social and political philosophy. That said, still happy to give this a shot!

Note first that morality comes in degrees. Actions are more or less ethical or unethical, more or less morally permissible or impermissible, more or less morally praiseworthy, objectionable, questionable, etc. So I won't be offering a binary "yes it was ethical" or "no it was unethical" analysis that suggests that all actions on one side or the other are on par with one another. I suspect you accept as much – just clarifying.

Ethics in a Nutshell Chapter 2: What's "Ethics"?
Matt Deaton
6 months ago
How philosophical ethics -- the reason-based attempt to answer life's big non-empirical questions -- can be complementary to...

Ethics in a Nutshell Chapter 5: The Four Dominant Ethical Theories
Matt Deaton
6 months ago
Brief intro to Kantianism, Utilitarianism, Feminist Care Ethics and Virtue Ethics.

Ethics in a Nutshell Chapter 7: Argument by Analogy
Matt Deaton
6 months ago
What are arguments by analogy? Why are they so effective? What does a violinist have to do with the ethics of abortion?

Ethics in a Nutshell Chapter 9: Conclusion
Matt Deaton
6 months ago
Book wrap-up lecture near Times Square. Yelling does not imply anger, and product appearances do not imply endorsement

ETHICS IN A NUTSHELL

THE PHILOSOPHER'S APPROACH TO MORALITY IN 100 PAGES

Matt Deaton, Ph.D.

Ethics in a Nutshell: The Philosopher's Approach to Morality in 100 Pages

ISBN 978-0-9892542-4-3

Published by Notaed Press, Vonore, TN

Cover art "Human Pods" by Ashley Addair of
AshleyDawnAddair.com

Acknowledgments

Thanks to Ben Masaoka, ethics bowl coach at Roosevelt High School in Seattle, Kelsey Walker, ethics bowl undergraduate intern at the Center for Philosophy for Children at Washington University, Roberta Israeloff, friend and former colleague at the Squire Family Foundation, Jennifer Everett, philosophy professor at DePauw University in Indiana, Andrew Petti, ethics bowl competitor at Dwight-Englewood School in New Jersey, and Allison Kelley, teacher and ethics bowl coach at Avon High School in Indiana for reviewing and making helpful edit suggestions on previous versions of *Nutshell*. Special thanks to renowned Barnard College, University of Columbia professor of political theory, Dennis Dalton, for encouragement and insights, especially on the Virtue Ethics section.

Thanks to mentors and former University of Tennessee Philosophy Department chairs, John Hardwig and David Reidy, for first giving me the chance to teach ethics on the university level.

Thanks to head coach Lance McConkey and the Sequoyah High School Ethics Bowl team for reviewing this manuscript, and for allowing me the pleasure of being your assistant coach (go, Chiefs!).

And special thanks to talented friend and former student, Ashley Addair, for this beautiful cover. May everyone judge *Nutshell* by it.

For students brave enough to study ethics in good faith.

Contents

Chapter 1

Introduction

Philosophers tend to write for other philosophers. The style and terminology of academic ethics can therefore seem uninviting. However, everything professional ethicists discuss and do can be broken down into simple concepts any bright teenager can comprehend.

Whether you're here out of curiosity or for a class, studying the philosopher's approach to morality is likely to heighten your moral sense and reveal the complexity of what once seemed clear and simple. As this complexity unfolds, you may find some of your current views less defendable than you once thought, which can be a little scary.

Doing ethics honestly and with an open mind therefore requires courage. Not firefighter courage. But courage nonetheless.

If you're interested in developing a more nuanced, rich and mature understanding of right and wrong, and if the thought of holding a set of moral beliefs that can withstand scrutiny is appealing, you've come to the right place. But know that ninety-eight pages from now, you're likely to be a slightly different person.

Fans of *The Matrix* might liken this to Morpheus's red pill warning to Neo: "Remember, all I'm offering is the truth. Nothing more." Neo's truth was that he was living in a computer simulation. I hope any truth you uncover here is much less dramatic. But studying ethics can prove discomforting, so buckle up.

NUTSHELL IN A NUTSHELL

I wrote the first version of *Nutshell* for students in my applied ethics courses at the University of Tennessee where I had the pleasure of teaching Contemporary Moral

Issues, Business Ethics, Professional Responsibility, Social and Political Philosophy, and Bioethics—first as a graduate teaching associate, and also briefly as a fulltime lecturer. I later expanded and revised a similar version to share with the ethics bowl community, tweaked that version for my students at the University of Texas at Tyler, and most recently revised once again after recording YouTube lectures for each of the chapters (several in my home, one floating down a river, and a handful at landmarks in New York). You can access these videos by clicking on the chapter titles if you're reading this on your Kindle, or if you're holding the print book, by visiting EthicsinaNutshell.org.

Nutshell covers the basics of any good introductory college ethics course: what academic philosophy is, why philosophical ethics is compatible with religious moral reasoning, problems with moral subjectivism (or the view that morality is a mere matter of personal opinion), the four dominant ethical theories of

Kantianism, Utilitarianism, Virtue Ethics and Feminist Care Ethics, the role of our moral intuitions, how to construct and evaluate moral arguments (especially moral arguments by analogy), how careful moral reflection can produce a more coherent and logically defensible set of moral views, and how to arrive at an "All-Things-Considered" view that balances and takes into account all of the above.

The goal of *Nutshell* isn't to tell you what to think about various ethical and political issues, or to even replace whatever method you currently use to decide them. Rather, its modest aim is to introduce you to the philosopher's approach to morality with the hope that you'll find some of it worth making your own.

THE BASIC BUILDING BLOCKS

Academic philosophy is the reason-based attempt to answer life's big, non-empirical questions, "non-empirical" simply meaning not directly measurable in the physical world. *Nutshell* focuses on ethics, which is but one of the four sub-disciplines of philosophy, the other three being logic (the study of the basic rules of reason, progress in which enabled the advent of computer coding), metaphysics (the study of the ultimate nature of the universe, which goes beyond observable science) and epistemology (the study of what constitutes genuine knowledge, which is sometimes oversimplified as justified true belief).

I describe academic philosophy as the "reason-based" attempt to answer questions in these areas because philosophers use logic to form arguments, which are composed of a series of claims, called premises, intended to logically support another claim, called the conclusion. Notice that "argument" and "conclusion" are used in special, technical ways in this context, the former *not* referring to a quarrel between two people, and the latter *not* referring to the end of a story. An argument could very well be fully presented by a single author, and a conclusion could be stated at the outset of an argument.

Most philosophers' styles are more subtle, but anytime you read or hear the words "therefore" or "thus," a conclusion is likely nearby. Similarly, the words "because" or "since" commonly indicate premises. For example, here's a deceptively simple ethical argument:

> *Because* normal adult mammals can experience pleasure and pain, their interests *therefore* deserve consideration.

On the surface, we have an observation hastily followed by a declaration. But this is actually a very complex argument waiting to be unpacked and examined. It rests on dozens of implicit premises concerning why the ability to experience pleasure and pain (or "sentience") is morally significant, why moral significance is tied to an obligation to acknowledge and respect interests, and even what "interests," "deserves" and other key terms really mean.

Part Scientist, Part Vulcan

Members of the philosophical community (which you are hereby invited to join) construct, share, evaluate and revise arguments like the example above in a collective effort to make moral progress, similar to how the scientific community uses hypotheses, experiments, observation and analysis to make scientific progress. Given that arguments are our basic building blocks, we consider conceptual clarity and precision super important, much like how scientists consider the precision and accuracy of their instruments and calculations super important.

Another similarity between philosophers and scientists is that just like any good scientist, any good philosopher is willing to change his or her mind on most any issue if given good enough reason to do so. In both cases, evidence (in the scientist's case, empirical and measurable; in our case, abstract and conceptual) is paramount. Both scientists and philosophers are obliged to conclude as the balance of evidence suggests.

This doesn't mean that scientists and philosophers don't possess strongly-held views. It just means that they recognize their fallibility, and strive to align themselves with what seems most logically defensible—most consistent with the best reasons and evidence—regardless of what they presently happen to think. Good scientists and philosophers are therefore simultaneously smart and humble, which is a stark contrast with the one-sided, *defend-your-view-to-the-death* approach modeled by attorneys, politicians and advocates of various causes you're apt to see on television or the web.

If a movie character would help, think of *Star Trek's* Spock. He's serious, logical, and very confident in his reasoning ability. But at the same time his devotion to truth requires that he remain open to new information, and always willing to change his mind.

An adolescent Spock actually recites the definition of the philosophical ethical term "supererogatory" during a flashback of his schooling in the 2009 film. As juvenile Spock put it, an action is supererogatory "when it is morally praiseworthy, but not morally obligatory." Moments later he pummels bullies for insulting his human mother, and later exacts revenge on time-traveling Romulans for destroying his home planet.

But that's enough Trekkie nerdishness... for now. Before we cover some important distinctions between morality, psychology, predictability and legality, and then review the four dominant ethical theories, we should first unpack what the term "ethics" even means. Or at least what it means when philosophers use it.

So welcome to the world of philosophical ethics. Whether this is your first or simply your latest adventure into academic philosophy, I hope you enjoy the journey. And be sure to check out those videos, which are designed to reinforce key concepts we'll cover in greater depth here.

Chapter 2

What's "Ethics"?

The United States Senate has an "ethics" committee, many companies have official "ethics" codes, and attorneys are required to take "ethics" training. But when academic philosophers use the term, they're referring to the reason-guided study of what we morally ought to do.

This isn't to say that senators, companies and lawyers don't use reason (most certainly do), or don't make decisions about what we morally ought to do (most certainly try). It just means that what distinguishes the philosopher's approach is that the ultimate grounding for their views is reason itself, as opposed to voter preferences, company policy, or legal precedent.

PHILOSOPHICAL ETHICS, RELIGION, AND PUBLIC DISCOURSE

Religious persons are sometimes suspicious of this reason-centric approach to morality, and worry that thinking through ethical questions from any perspective other than a religious perspective might be disrespectful to their faith. However, many professional philosophers are devoutly religious, and many religious professionals are well-studied in philosophy. Some segregate their personal religious convictions from their philosophical reasoning, keeping the two mentally separate. "Reason leads me to conclude X," they might think, "but my faith leads me to conclude *not* X."

How people reconcile conflicts between their non-religious and religious views is of course up to them. I personally use philosophy to inform my religious understanding and vice versa. Along with many others, I figure if a creator gave us these big brains, he, she, or it would expect and want us to use them—not only

12

to better understand the natural world for scientific and technological purposes, but the moral world so we can make better decisions.

Therefore it would perhaps be a waste, and maybe even a dishonor, if we didn't utilize our intellectual abilities to think through life's big questions (which is what philosophers do generally), including big questions concerning what we morally ought to do. You're of course free to use the philosopher's approach to morality however you see fit. You might just entertain it for the purposes of the class, if that's why you're here. The point is simply that philosophy isn't necessarily hostile to religion. In fact, many believe the two can be quite complementary.

ENABLING INTER-FAITH DIALOGUE

One benefit of being able to think through moral and political issues from a philosophical perspective is that it facilitates conversation with virtually anyone, whereas only being able to reason from a religious perspective limits deliberation partners to those who happen to share your faith. For example, if in discussing the death penalty I assert a position that rests on a key passage from the New Testament, my argument may impress Christians, but it isn't likely to convince an Agnostic, Jew, Buddhist, Muslim, Atheist, Hindu, or any other non-Christian. These persons may respect the content of the New Testament insofar as they acknowledge that it is important to and carries weight for me. But from their perspective, it would have little further authority.

Similarly, if someone were to respond to my position (my *current* position—remember that good philosophers are always willing to change their minds) on the death penalty by citing the Koran, their point would have little purchase, for I'm not Muslim. I would recognize that they consider the book holy, and respect its content insofar as I respect them. But scripture from the Koran doesn't carry nearly the same weight for non-Muslims as it does for Muslims.

Thankfully, philosophical ethics can facilitate discussion amongst persons from a variety of backgrounds, committed to a variety of religious and areligious perspectives. This is because philosophical ethics utilizes considerations almost everyone recognizes as morally relevant, and the fact that philosophers judge reasons and arguments based on their logical force, rather than their consistency with a particular religious tradition.

This ability to transcend "comprehensive doctrines" enables discussion and moral progress where it might otherwise flounder, which is especially useful for those of us living in multicultural societies, where we risk disrespecting our fellow citizens when our policy preferences are not based in reasons a multitude of diverse others can appreciate.

Christian philosopher Robert Audi has argued that thinking through issues from a "public" perspective, using reasons anyone should be able to appreciate, regardless of their religious commitments of lack thereof, seems required by the Golden Rule—that doing so is a matter of treating others the way we would like to be treated. To evaluate Audi's argument, just ask yourself, "Were I a member of a religious minority, would I want laws governing my behavior justified by and based on a religion of which I'm not a member?"

Whether you find Audi's argument compelling, an important question for any student of ethics is whether genuine reason-based progress can be made concerning moral matters in the first place. Isn't morality, as pop culture often suggests, simply a matter of personal taste? Aren't we all entitled to our moral opinions, with each being equally valuable and immune from criticism? Aren't ethical views just like ice cream flavors in that we all have our favorites, but none are really *better* than the others?

Chapter 3

Why Ethics Isn't Ice Cream

While citing religious texts is a popular way to answer moral questions, many people refer to their upbringing, reflect on their society's values, and in tough cases simply flip a coin. "Heads and the death penalty is sometimes morally permissible—tails and the death penalty is never morally permissible." Most of us mix these approaches, drawing on our religious understanding, familial and social values, and flipping coins as a last resort.

Philosophers, on the other hand, insist that we use reason to answer ethical questions. Why? Because reason has proven itself reliable in answering other sorts of questions.

For example, scientists don't rely on traditional knowledge or public opinion polls when uncovering the complexities of the natural world. If they did, we might still believe the earth is flat. Rather, they gather evidence, examine reasons for and against hypotheses, and draw conclusions based on their logical force.

Philosophers use reason in a similar way. The difference is that while scientists concern themselves with empirical questions and enjoy the luxury of testable data, philosophers concern themselves with non-empirical questions for which irrefutable evidence is usually unavailable.

For example, the temperature of a planet's surface can be measured with a thermometer, and a meteor can be examined for traces of DNA using an electron microscope. There's no arguing with a thermometer or microscope: the average temperature on Mars is either -67 degrees Fahrenheit or it's not; that meteor your lucky cousin found either contains traces of DNA or it doesn't. These are questions we can conclusively answer by examining the physical world.

However, determining whether and to what extent an action is morally obligatory, morally permissible (allowed but optional), morally impermissible (forbidden or simply wrong), etc. is a less straightforward endeavor. No "goodometer" or "moralscope" can decide for us whether mining minerals on Mars or cloning DNA sequences found on a meteor would be ethically OK.

This lack of a way to measure moral questions makes moral views more contentious. Without the benefit of a goodometer or moralscope it's more difficult to decisively settle disagreements among people with conflicting views—and boy, do people seem to hold conflicting views!

But does this mean there's no such thing as moral right and wrong? Does it mean ethics, morality—what we ought to do—is all just a matter of personal opinion?

A Negative Argument

People sometimes hastily conclude that since ethical questions can't be empirically proven one way or the other, and since there seems to be much disagreement over whether certain actions are morally permissible, ethics must be a subjective matter—something that depends on personal perspective, similar to which flavor of ice cream is most delicious.

Philosophers agree that which flavor of ice cream is most delicious is indeed a subjective matter. That is, the answer really does depend on whom you ask, and how they happen to perceive the interaction of their taste buds with the different chemicals in the different flavors.

Accordingly, it makes perfect sense to say, "Chocolate is the most delicious flavor of ice cream *for Matt*," and simultaneously say, "Vanilla is the most delicious flavor of ice cream *for Lisa*." These personalized statements are consistent with the nature of taste. However, most philosophers reject the idea that ethics is similarly subjective for two main reasons.

First, simply because a question can't be empirically proven doesn't mean it doesn't have an objective (external, non-perspective based) answer. Take, for example, whether intelligent life exists beyond Earth. This is something current technology can't conclusively confirm or refute. Maybe there are smart aliens out there— maybe there aren't. Right now we can't know for sure.

Those who have studied the issue disagree. Some scientists have concluded that intelligent life does most likely exist beyond Earth, and some have concluded that it most likely does not. Imagine that: equally intelligent people examining the same evidence and reaching conflicting conclusions. Does this mean whether intelligent life exists beyond Earth is a subjective matter, similar to which flavor of ice cream is most delicious?

Of course not. Intelligent life either exists beyond Earth or it doesn't. This fact neither depends on our ability to know for sure nor on what scientists happen to think. In fact, even if every scientist were in complete agreement on the matter, the objective facts would not change—smart aliens do not pop in and out of existence depending on whether people happen to believe in them.

Consider how humans once believed the earth was flat. Our ancestors' confidence that it was flat didn't make it flat any more than our confidence that it's spherical makes it spherical. Planets are flat, spherical or some other shape independent of what humans happen to believe, for beliefs are simply mind states, which usually have little direct bearing on reality.

Therefore it wouldn't make sense to say, "Intelligent life exists beyond earth, *for Dr. Smith*," or "Intelligent life does not exist beyond earth, *for Dr. Jones*." These personalized claims are inconsistent with the objective nature of existing, being alive, and being intelligent.

We might instead say that Dr. Smith and

Dr. Jones disagree over whether intelligent life exists beyond earth, and given current technologies, we can't know for sure who is correct. But recognizing their disagreement and our inability to confirm who is correct is very different from concluding that facts concerning the object of their inquiry turn on personal taste.

Similarly, the fact that we can't conclusively settle disagreements over ethical matters doesn't mean these are matters of subjective opinion either. Dr. Smith and Dr. Jones may disagree just as vehemently over whether (and under what circumstances) abortions are morally permissible as they disagree over the existence of intelligent alien life. And in both cases, we may lack a fully conclusive way to determine who is correct. But that disagreement and our inability to conclusively settle it doesn't mean the moral permissibility of abortion is any more a matter of opinion than the existence of smart aliens.

A POSITIVE ARGUMENT

The above is an example of what philosophers sometimes call a "negative" argument—one that refutes a line of reasoning for a competing conclusion, rather than providing reasons to accept the conclusion you ultimately aim to support. In this case we refuted the argument that moral disagreement implies moral subjectivism (or the whole "ethics is personal opinion" thing), but that does little to show the alternative of moral objectivism (or the view that morality rests on some firmer basis) is necessarily true.

However, there is one very strong, albeit very simple, positive argument that gives us reason to believe ethical questions do indeed possess objective answers, and are most definitely not mere matters of personal opinion. And that argument concerns the ridiculous consequences of believing otherwise.

If we were to believe that moral questions were a matter of personal opinion, similar to which flavor of ice cream is most delicious, logical consistency would require that we endorse the claim that virtually *any* action is morally permissible.

Subjectivism isn't a big deal when we're talking about ice cream. If Johnny sincerely believes *skunk oil* is the most delicious flavor, that's odd, but who cares—Johnny's just a weirdo, and we can respect his tastes…from a distance. However, what if Johnny's moral beliefs are just as repugnant? What if he sincerely believes it's morally permissible to torture babies for fun? Johnny doesn't have in mind scenarios where he's forced to choose between torturing a baby or some greater evil, such as allowing a madman to detonate a nuclear bomb in the middle of a crowded city. No, Johnny believes that torturing any baby at any time for any reason is completely morally acceptable—even if one does it just for kicks.

Here's the problem: when we equate ethics with ice cream, we have to agree that if

Johnny really believes torturing babies for fun is morally permissible, torturing babies for fun *really is* morally permissible, at least for Johnny.

But our good sense tells us that torturing babies for fun is clearly immoral, no matter how sincerely Johnny might believe it to be morally OK. While moral subjectivism might be tacitly endorsed by those who haven't given the issue much thought, a moment's reflection shows that its implications are completely inconsistent with our most fundamental notions of ethical right and wrong.

Moral subjectivism also facilitates a dangerous sort of arrogance. Suppose Johnny decides to torture *you* for fun. Were he a moral subjectivist, Johnny would have little reason to feel guilty. Were you to challenge him, he might simply remind you how sincerely he believes torturing you is morally OK, and even amplify the torture to demonstrate his certitude. But perhaps even worse, were *you* a moral subjectivist, you could protest and complain, but not on ethical grounds. You could beg for mercy, but could not protest that the torture was *evil* or *wrong* or *immoral*. For so long as Johnny believed his actions were morally OK, as a moral subjectivist, you'd have to agree that they were indeed morally OK, at least for Johnny. (One has to wonder how quickly Johnny would abandon subjectivism were the roles reversed!)

REJECTING CULTURAL SUBJECTIVISM, TOO

We now have two strong arguments in favor of rejecting moral subjectivism. First, the fact that we can't conclusively settle disagreement over ethical questions doesn't make ethics a matter of personal opinion any more than it makes questions concerning the existence of intelligent aliens a matter of personal opinion. And second, endorsing moral subjectivism would entail the absurd implication that whatever any person happened to believe is ethical would in fact be ethical...for them—

repugnant examples of which conflict with our fundamental understanding of right and wrong.

At this point you might wonder if rather than grounding morality in personal opinion it might be better to ground morality in cultural or societal opinion. Though a common strategy, the same considerations that led us to conclude ethics can't be a matter of personal taste give us good reason to conclude ethics can't be a matter of cultural taste, either.

For example, even if every last person in Afghanistan believed it was immoral to educate women, that wouldn't mean educating women (even women in Afghanistan) was in fact immoral. Though biologically different in obvious ways, women and men share in their yearning and potential for learning, which would make allowing schooling for one but not the other difficult to justify, regardless of how a culture might be in unison on the matter.

Notice that the same is true of positions which we have good independent reason to endorse. For example, America's constitutional democratic system of basic rights, equal protection under the law, separation of powers and presumption of innocence until proven guilty seems a just way for rational creatures to self-govern. But it's a system of government worthy of our rational assent not because we happen to like it, but due to these and other justifying reasons. Hate it or love it, it's good or bad independent of our collective view.

Of course, every last citizen of the United States isn't committed to our system of government any more than every Afghan believes it's immoral to educate women—no social group in the real world agrees 100% on much of anything. The point is that even if Afghans and Americans were respectively unanimous, their agreement wouldn't serve as an infallible source of moral truth, any more than it would serve as an infallible source of scientific truth. Just because a culture sincerely believes a practice or institution is ethically just, unjust, permissible, impermissible, forbidden or obligatory doesn't necessarily make it so.

And so we have good reason to reject moral subjectivism and endorse some version of moral objectivism: the view that ethical questions have answers that do not depend on an individual or a culture's beliefs. Keep in mind that this doesn't mean we necessarily possess those answers. It simply means they're out there, somewhere, apparently independent of what people happen to believe.

Philosophers have thought long and hard about how to best discover these answers, and have developed several theories along the way. But before we explore and begin applying Kantianism, Utilitarianism, Virtue Ethics and Feminist Care Ethics, we should review three key distinctions that often confuse people new to philosophical ethics.

CHAPTER 4

THREE KEY DISTINCTIONS

PRESCRIPTIVE VS. PREDICTIVE

When your dentist tells you that brushing your teeth twice per day *should* prevent cavities, he's making a prediction. "Do x and y *should* (or is likely to) follow." However, if he said you *should* donate your toothbrush to a homeless person, this would be less about predicting your behavior and more about doing what's morally right. "You *should* do x because it's the morally right thing to do."

Hopefully he'd provide an argument to support such a claim—even if we had an obligation to provide the less fortunate with toothbrushes, gifting new ones would seem equally effective and much less gross. My point is simply to illustrate how the word "should" can be used in both a predictive and a prescriptive way. "Ought" can be used similarly.

If I say the Vols (the college football team from Knoxville, Tennessee) *ought* to beat the Gators (the college football team from Gainesville, Florida) this season, I'm making a statement about which team I expect to win as a matter of predicting the future, not a statement about how a Vol loss would somehow be immoral (although losses to the Gators often *feel* vaguely immoral to many Vol fans).

However, if I said that fans on both sides *ought* to boycott the Tennessee/Florida game to protest the mounting evidence that football causes serious brain injuries over time, that's an ethical statement about doing what's right, not a prediction about what the fans will actually do.

So remember: "should" and "ought" can indicate an expected future state or a moral obligation. And since ethics is all about doing what's right, philosophers typically use the terms in their prescriptive or evaluative sense rather than their predictive sense.

MORALITY VS. PSYCHOLOGY

Imagine that a loved one is dying of a rare disease and the only medicine that can save her is too expensive for you or your family to afford. If you had no other way to save her, would it be morally permissible for you steal the medicine?

Before you answer, notice that I didn't ask if placed in such a situation whether you *would* steal the medicine. The question was whether you *should* steal the medicine. Predicting how you (or anyone) would be likely act under certain circumstances is distinct from how you *should* act if you're to do what's morally right. As philosophers, it's our job to figure out what should be done, even if the majority of people would likely behave differently.

Similarly, because everyone has told a lie and some people have committed murder doesn't mean lying or murder are morally permissible. Put another way, an *is* doesn't make an *ought*.

So be sure to separate likelihood or psychological propensity from morality. Though the two may be related, they are not the same.

MORALITY VS. LEGALITY

A third key distinction is that legal does not necessarily equal moral, and moral does not necessarily equal legal. As my philosophy of law professor David Reidy used to say, "Good law *tracks* morality, but doesn't guarantee it."

What Dr. Reidy meant was that in most cases we desire our laws to be ethically just. But simply because something is legally allowed doesn't mean it's morally permissible, and simply because something is legally forbidden doesn't mean it's immoral. This becomes pretty obvious when we notice how laws differ according to time and location.

For example, as of this writing, it is legally permissible to smoke marijuana for recreational purposes in Colorado, but in Vermont it is not.

In contrast, it is currently legally permissible for physicians to facilitate assisted suicides in Vermont, but in Colorado helping a patient hasten their death would get a doctor arrested.

Surely if I were to take off from an airport in Denver, CO and land in Montpelier, VT the moral status of recreational marijuana use and physician-assisted suicide wouldn't somehow magically switch mid-air.

Further, consider Oregon—a state in which both physician-assisted suicide and recreational marijuana smoking are legal, and Texas—a state in which both physician-assisted suicide and recreational marijuana smoking are illegal. Imagine if my plane took off from Denver, refueled in Portland, then traveled to Dallas (or Tyler), then to Montpelier and back via some different route.

It would certainly make sense to say that physician-assisted suicide and recreational marijuana use became *legal* and *illegal* depending on my location, for the legal status of an activity changes from geographical jurisdiction to jurisdiction. But it wouldn't seem to make much sense at all to say that physician-assisted suicide or recreational marijuana use changed from *moral* to *immoral* and back again depending on where I happened to be.

Note how this relates to the problem of cultural subjectivism from last chapter. Laws are often based on some imperfect approximation of cultural views, which are usually an imperfect aggregation of personal views, which could go in obviously unacceptable directions. We're assuming the people and governments of Colorado, Vermont, Oregon, and Texas have good reason for their conflicting regulations on recreational marijuana use and physician-assisted suicide. But imagine a state or nation full of citizens holding obviously immoral views.

If I flew to a Taliban-controlled region of Afghanistan, would it suddenly become *immoral* to educate women? It might become *illegal*, but surely not immoral. It's of course questionable how well Taliban leaders represent the views of the Afghan people. But the point is simply that cultural views, and the laws they support, are subject to the same flaws as personal views, and therefore neither personal taste, nor cultural norm, nor legal statute serve as a firm foundation for morality.

Yet another problem with conflating legality and morality is that if legality determined morality, genuine legal *progress* would be difficult, if not impossible. Just like the moral subjectivist being held prisoner in Johnny's basement couldn't object on moral grounds, those who would base morality on legality would have to accept what the law currently *is*, with little principled reason to change it. I suppose they could advocate for their self-interests, just like the subjectivist prisoner in Johnny's basement could beg for mercy. But they couldn't say that this or that law should be made more ethically just.

Thankfully, most everyone tacitly agrees,

and people do advocate to make laws morally better. Which changes would constitute improvements and whether citizens and officials are successful in making laws more ethically just are separate matters. But the point here is simply that morality precedes legality, not the other way around.

America's founding fathers realized this, and that's one reason our Constitution includes not only a process whereby laws can be changed, but even a process whereby the Constitution itself can be changed. That's what "amendments" are, and presumably even the Constitution's amendment procedures could themselves be amended.

Therefore, don't look to the law for your morals—not even to the Constitution. Rather than deferring to what currently happens to be legal or illegal, it's our job as ethicists, and simply as citizens, to figure out what the law *should* be. That doesn't mean we don't have some moral obligation to obey current law, or that law has absolutely no moral standing. Most philosophers would say that a law's moral force increases to the extent that it seems to track objective morality, and to the extent that it's the result of a democratic process in a just society. It simply means that we shouldn't fall into the trap of thinking legality equals morality. Good law tracks morality, not necessarily the other way around.

You now have a taste of how philosophers use argumentation to think through life's big non-empirical questions. You have good reason to think morality isn't a mere matter of personal opinion. And with these three distinctions out of the way you're finally ready to explore the four dominant ethical theories.

If a ten-minute primer might help, now's a good time to watch my YouTube video on chapter 5. And as I say in the vid, there's a lot to these theories we're leaving out, so don't be afraid to do some additional research if you find one especially interesting.

Chapter 5

The Four Dominant Ethical Theories

Four theories dominate contemporary philosophical ethics: Kantianism, Consequentialism (of which Utilitarianism is the most popular version), Virtue Ethics and Feminist Care Ethics. Each is supported by a rich literature filled with intricate nuance. What we'll cover here is only a bird's eye view of each, with abbreviated versions of each theory's respective supporting argument.

Philosophers disagree over which theory enjoys the strongest logical support. But as we'll see, each promotes a basic component of human morality virtually anyone can appreciate and take seriously, regardless of their culture, religion, location or place in history. Those basic moral components and their associated theories are respect for persons and rational consistency (Kantianism), outcomes, pleasure, and pain (Consequentialism or Utilitarianism), character (Virtue Ethics), and relationships (Feminist Care Ethics).

KANTIANISM

He's been dead for 200 years, but philosophers remain in awe of the brilliance of German philosopher Immanuel Kant. With lasting influence in all four corners of philosophy (logic, epistemology, metaphysics and ethics), his impact on ethics is perhaps most profound.

Kant argued that what gives persons intrinsic, infinite value is their ability to reason. Our capacity for higher reason facilitates most everything we do, distinguishes us from nonhuman animals, and gives us the freedom to live lives that are genuinely our own. Like no other Earthly creature, human beings can reflect on their personality, character, and lives, decide to change them, form a plan, and take steps to make their vision reality. It's our capacity of reason that enables this unique freedom or "autonomy."

Further, without reason we couldn't properly value anything. That is, we couldn't decide which things are more or less important without considering whether, how, and to what extent they align with our goals and commitments. And all of that involves abstract thought—aka reasoning. So since valuing requires reasoning, if we value anything at all, we ought to value reason itself. Kant argued that properly valuing reason entails following two rules, which form the heart of Kantian Ethics. Those two rules are:

1. *Only do things you could rationally endorse everyone else doing in similar circumstances.*
2. *Always treat persons with respect, and never as mere tools.*

43

The first rule, sometimes called the first formulation of the "Categorical Imperative" (a fancy term that simply means a rule you should always follow, regardless of your immediate aims), precludes lying, stealing, murdering and the like, for those are actions you couldn't endorse everyone else doing in relevantly similar circumstances. This is because if _everyone_ lied, stole or murdered, we wouldn't gain anything by doing those things ourselves.

Imagine a world in which people always lied when it was to their advantage. What would happen? Lots of things, but at root, if people always lied, the social convention of trust, which is based on the expectation that people generally tell the truth, would dissolve. This would mean no one would ever take anyone at their word, and therefore there would be no benefit to lying. If I skipped work to go to a ballgame, then tried to convince my boss that I was out sick, she wouldn't believe me if everyone _always_ lied. If I blew my family's grocery budget on a new

Spyderco knife, then tried to convince them I lost the money in a robbery, they wouldn't believe me if everyone *always* lied. Lying may be personally beneficial when it is rare. But if people did it *all* the time, lying would be pretty useless.

You might ask, what if people only lied under extreme circumstances? Couldn't we universalize lying when, say, there's an axe murderer at the door trying to get in? Actually, no! If everyone always lied when axe murderers were at their door, well, axe murderers wouldn't believe us when we tried to trick them. "Sorry, Mr. Axe Murderer—nobody's home." "I know better than that!" *<bursts through door with axe>* Kant himself realized as much, and maintained that the best an ethical person could do in such a situation would be to lock their door and remain silent.

Remember that the question isn't what we'd personally be willing to tolerate or what we'd like to do. It's whether universalizing the action would undermine the advantage we're tempted to seek (such as getting away with skipping work, or avoiding a murderer's axe).

Theft is similarly non-universalizable. Just imagine a world in which people always stole when it was to their advantage. If the tools I use to accomplish my goals—my laptop, my bicycle, my raft—were constantly being taken, living a productive, meaningful life would be very difficult. I'd spend most of my time securing and reacquiring my stuff, with little time left for writing, family bike rides, or floats down the Hiwassee River.

Further, in a world in which everyone always stole, whatever we were able to steal would quickly be stolen, making our original theft quite useless. And apart from being frustrating and pointless, constant widespread theft would make a vibrant economy impossible, for if retailers weren't paid for their inventory and producers weren't paid for their goods, both would quickly go out of business.

As we can see, when considering whether

an action is consistent with Kantian Ethics, the first thing we should ask ourselves is whether universalizing it would somehow undermine the benefit or advantage we seek. (Do this for downloading pirated movies on your own now. What answer did you reach? Why?) Kant would say that if you can't endorse everyone else doing something in similar circumstances, it must be somehow irrational, and is therefore unethical.

However, even if the action you're considering passes this first test, you're not cleared just yet. You still need to run it through the second formulation of the Categorical Imperative (or just that second rule above), and ask whether it shows all involved rational parties adequate respect.

Kant's mandate that we show persons adequate respect and never treat them as mere tools is based on his emphasis on our rationality. It's completely fine to abuse a hammer without regard to its welfare, for a hammer can't think, decide, or carry out a life plan. As an inanimate object, a hammer has no interests, and is only instrumentally valuable—valuable only insofar as it can do something for us.

The carpenter who swings that hammer, on the other hand, can indeed think, decide, and carry out a life plan. She is a rational, autonomous agent, and has many interests, with many goals and aspirations. The same is true for you and me. As creatures with complex interests and plans, we desire and expect that others will honor them, and not interfere with them without good reason. It is therefore incumbent upon us to treat one another not as simple objects, valuable only insofar as we can provide one another some benefit—but as fellow reasoners with intrinsic worth.

What exactly this entails has been interpreted differently by different philosophers. Some Kantians argue that treating others with respect mainly entails refraining from doing them harm. However, other Kantians argue that treating persons with respect requires actively helping them when in need and looking out for their best interests.

In the Business Ethics literature, for example, some argue that Kantian respect for persons simply involves being up front with employees about working conditions and ensuring that they freely agree to their employment contracts. This would mean that if a job involved swimming in a cage with live sharks, an employer would need to ensure applicants and employees were aware of the danger, but needn't do anything to mitigate it.

Others argue that fully respecting employees requires providing a living wage, a safe working environment, and reasonably interesting work, or at least not *mind-numbing* work. This would mean shark swimmers should not only be informed of the danger, but provided with safety equipment, and enough pay to cover basic housing, nutrition and health care. (No one can complain that shark swimmers have boring jobs!) Which of these interpretations of this second component of Kantian Ethics is most convincing I leave to you to decide. Which seems to best show rational agents adequate respect? Why?

UTILITARIANISM

While Kantianism mandates that we never lie or steal, Consequentialism actually *requires* that we lie and steal when doing so will bring about the best overall future. According to Consequentialist ethical theory, a person's actions aren't judged based on whether they show others proper respect or are consistent with a universalizability test, but instead according to the consequences they produce.

Utilitarianism, famously popularized by 18th and 19th century English philosophers Jeremy Bentham and John Stuart Mill, is the most common breed of Consequentialism. Utilitarians argue that we have a moral mandate to specifically bring about the consequence of maximized net pleasure, and should choose actions based on their likelihood of producing that aim. This is because pleasure seems to be the only thing valued for its own sake, and there's no reason to think any particular creature's pursuit of it is any more important than the next's. Maximizing net pleasure is therefore a way to treat all creatures with equal respect—everyone's pleasure and pain count the same in the "Utilitarian calculus."

Let's first consider the Utilitarian premise that pleasure is the only thing valued for its own sake. A Utilitarian would argue that you no doubt value your toothbrush, but only instrumentally—only because it enables some additional valued result. Namely, your toothbrush keeps your teeth clean and healthy, so it's clean, healthy teeth that you really value, not your toothbrush, right? Actually, a Utilitarian would argue that you don't value your teeth for their own sake either. You value them for their ability to help you consume food, or maybe insofar as their cleanliness is integral to your attractiveness, but in any case, not for their own sake. Further, not even food is valuable for its own sake. We value our food for the pleasure its consumption produces, and for the nutrition it provides, enabling us to maintain a pleasurable state, and otherwise seek out pleasure in ways only healthy people can. So it's the direct experience of *pleasure* that you value at root—not your food, or your ability to chew it, or the cleanliness of your teeth, and definitely not your toothbrush.

This is true of everything, or so Utilitarians argue. Our smartphones, our Twitter accounts (@Matt_Deaton), our healthy bodies—*even our loved ones*—are all valued for the pleasure they ultimately facilitate, and not for their own sake. Go ahead and run this thought experiment on the things you value. Can you think of something you value for its own sake, and not for the pleasure it ultimately makes possible?

Assuming that this line of reasoning works, Utilitarians go on to argue that humans are equal in that we all seek to attain pleasure and avoid pain. We may do this in our own way—some by becoming stock brokers, accountants and philosophers, others by becoming priests, mothers and race car drivers. But whatever our path, pleasure is what we're after.

Given that we share that basic aim, there's no reason to think that any one person's pursuit of pleasure is more important than the next's. Therefore the morally right course of action is the one that brings about the most pleasure overall. Utilitarianism can thus be summarized:

> ➢ *Do whatever will maximize overall net pleasure.*

It's important to notice that the mandate isn't to maximize *your personal* pleasure. Utilitarianism isn't an excuse to do whatever's best for you regardless of the impact on others—

it isn't selfish egoism. In fact, devout Utilitarians will often sacrifice their own happiness for the sake of others when doing so will bring about more pleasure overall.

For example, if I'm a Utilitarian with a Snickers bar, and sharing it with you will bring about more pleasure overall than eating it myself, I have a moral obligation to do so. I might enjoy 4 units of pleasure if I eat it alone, and only 3 units of pleasure if I share. But if sharing will bring you more than 1 unit of pleasure, that will produce greater than 4 units total, which trumps the 4 units I'd enjoy if I kept it to myself.

This example seems pretty easy at first glance. But how can we tell *for sure* that sharing will produce the most net pleasure? After all, maybe the Snickers bar contains rotten peanuts, and instead of just making me sick, sharing it makes you sick, too! Now, vomiting side by side, we're both suffering extreme *displeasure*, whereas had I kept it to myself, only I would be sick.

Another problem is that judgments about

the pleasure or pain others experience are necessarily uncertain, for we can't "get inside" anyone else's head and experience the world from their perspective. Based on your expression of satisfaction and moans of chocolate ecstasy, I may *think* that you enjoy the Snickers bar as much as I do. But maybe 4 units of joy on your scale is only 0.4 units of joy on my scale—in which case maximizing overall pleasure would have required eating it all myself. *(4 units for me + 0 units for you) > (3 units for me + 0.4 units for you)*

These are serious worries with which Utilitarians continue to grapple. But they don't fully undercut the credibility or usefulness of the ethical theory. We naturally make rough utility judgments all the time, and doing so usually works acceptably well. Anytime we're presented with an ethical dilemma Utilitarianism says we should articulate our options, list everyone potentially impacted, consider the likely outcomes of the candidate actions, calculate the net pleasure each is likely to produce, and take whichever path most likely to maximize it.

To illustrate, imagine you're walking to Freshman English when you pass an apparent stab victim. He's bleeding badly, no one is stopping to help, and you know first aid. You also know your English teacher is giving a quiz at the beginning of next period, and that she doesn't allow make-ups under *any* circumstances. What should you do?

In deciding, first recognize that you have at least two options—go on to class or stop and help—with at least three parties potentially impacted: you, the stab victim, and the stab victim's mother. There are of course other options: you could apply a quick tourniquet, dial 9-11, and run to class. And there are of course other parties potentially affected: the stab victim's cousins, the student population, and even the assailant who will face greater jail time if the victim dies. We're just simplifying the equation to illustrate the method.

To further simplify things we'll quantify each person's pleasure/pain on a 20-point scale from -10 to +10. Let -10 represent unbearable, excruciating, long-lasting pain, +10 represent wonderful, euphoric, long-lasting pleasure, and 0 represent complete indifference, with everything in between representing some point on that continuum.

Option One: _go on to class._ If you go on to class, you'll take the quiz, do well if you studied, and avoid bloodying your clothes. So from your perspective, let's say that's +1. For the stab victim, they're going to continue to bleed, risk brain injury and death, and at the very least suffer compounded long-term psychological damage. Not only were they _stabbed_, but dozens of their peers refused to help them. So from their perspective, given the uncertainty of how bad off they'll be, let's call that a -7. For the stab victim's mother, if you don't stop, she may lose a child, which I'm told is one of the most devastating things that can happen to a parent. And at the very least, she'll be similarly distraught that no one stopped to aid her baby. So let's call that a -7 as well, for a total of -13 (your +1 minus 7 minus 7 more).

Option Two: _stop and help_. If you stop, you'll miss the quiz and ruin your favorite shirt, but the satisfaction you'll gain from saving a life will likely outweigh those comparatively trivial inconveniences. (Notice that we're running mini calculations for each party—the pain of a missed quiz versus the satisfaction of saving a life.) So from your perspective, let's call that a +5. For the stab victim, you'll at the very least partially restore their faith in mankind, prevent lasting damage from extreme blood loss, and might even save their life. However, they still had a really bad day... they still got _stabbed_. So their overall pleasure can't be too high, which we'll say is at -4. Last, the victim's mother will still be upset her baby was stabbed, but she'll be eternally grateful that _someone_ cared enough to save him, so we'll assign that a -4 as well, for a total of -3 (your +5 minus 4 minus 4 more).

	Go to Class	Stop & Help
You:	+1	+5
Stab Victim	-7	-4
Victim's Mom	-7	-4
Net Pleasure	-13	-3

According to our assumptions, which are of course uncertain and rough, it looks like Utilitarianism would recommend that you stop and help the stab victim, for doing so would bring about -3 units of net pleasure overall, as opposed to -13 units of net pleasure overall. Ideally students would leave their shanks at home and no one would get stabbed at all. But if it's happened and these are your options, the Utilitarian calculus says the ethical thing to do is stop and help.

I hope that's what seemed right according to your common sense moral judgment all along. Just like torturing babies for fun is clearly unethical, a human life clearly carries more moral weight than a quiz grade.

However, notice that the math might have come out differently if the person considering stopping wasn't you, but instead an incredibly selfish jerk. If someone cared a great deal about clothes and grades, and very little about human life, that might be enough for the scales to tip in the other direction, and for the Utilitarian calculus to recommend they go on to class. However, once we widen the scope of consideration and take into account the impact in terms of multiplied fear and anxiety a murdered peer would have on the student population, it is very unlikely that one person's fixation on GPA and fashion could overcome the negative impact on all others, no matter how big a jerk they happened to be.

Last, you may have noticed that the above process would likely prove tedious and impractical. *"Wait just one second, stab victim. Let me break out my calculator and decide whether I should help you...*" But luckily there are many rules of thumb we can follow in a pinch that tend to maximize net pleasure, such as tell the truth, honor others' property, and help those in need when doing so would cause comparatively minor inconvenience. Philosophers have traditionally distinguished between "Act" and "Rule" Utilitarianism based on whether one takes the time to run the Utilitarian calculus for every decision (Act Util), or follows those general rules of thumb, such as don't steal, tell the truth, don't unjustifiably kill anyone, that tend to maximize net pleasure when followed generally (Rule Util).

However, even if Utilitarianism can be made practical, some have complained that the Consequentialist approach to ethics neglects an essential component of being a moral creature. And that essential component concerns the obligations we owe our loved ones, independent of the pleasure or pain prioritizing their interests might bring about.

Feminist Care Ethics

Care Ethics was developed as a response to what self-defined feminist philosophers considered the cold, calculating "malestream" approach to morality. They argue that our relational ties to family and friends are of obvious moral importance—that it's an irrefutable truth about the human experience that relationships matter. And therefore any ethical theory that doesn't take relationships very seriously (for example, *all the rest*) is flawed.

Note that its title doesn't mean Feminist Care Ethics only applies to women. In fact, as a proud manly man, I can say Feminist Care Ethics is quite consistent with a masculine perspective. After all, protecting and otherwise caring for his family is the quintessential mark of the mature manly male (caveman grunt—*ugh, ugh!*).

Apart from our relationships just seeming intuitively important, Care Ethicists argue for the primacy of relational considerations because we're fundamentally interdependent creatures.

Though we like to entertain the fantasy that we're independent islands, nobody comes into the world, is successfully reared, or even survives without the help and cooperation of lots of other persons. Even hermits like authors depend on the good people at Amazon to facilitate sale of their books, as well as deliverymen to deliver them. All of this takes place in an economy involving thousands, all working and living and creating based on knowledge learned from, and institutions established by, previous generations.

And while our ability to live our lives depends largely on the cooperation of strangers, it's our parents, siblings, spouses, close friends and other loved ones who most directly facilitate our flourishing. They care for us when we're too young, too old, or too sick to care for ourselves, celebrate our victories, console us in our failures, and generally make life worth living.

So don't pretend we're not in this together, Care Ethicists argue. Acknowledge our shared interdependence, and to the extent that you're emotionally attached and indebted to a particular person, give their interests special priority. We might summarize the requirements of Feminist Care Ethics like this:

> *Prioritize the interests of loved ones.*

To see the clear contrast of this approach with Utilitarianism in particular, imagine that aliens have abducted you, your mother the corporate lawyer, and a cancer researcher. Demented as aliens are, they force you to choose who among you shall live: your mother or the cancer researcher.

From the Utilitarian perspective, unless your mom does something socially beneficial on the side, you should probably pick her to die and the researcher to live. There's at least a chance the researcher will heal cancer patients and as a result produce pleasure (or at least alleviate pain). But your mom, *the corporate lawyer*, probably maximizes net *pain* with her evil lawyering trickery! (Note that attorneys are the descendants of mercenary reasoners called "sophists" who were the ancient enemies of philosophers. So nothing personal against your sweet mom—it's a philosopher thing. If you're a pre-law major, it's not too late!)

But Care Ethicists would object that your relationship with your mother should override the potential benefits saving the researcher instead. Beyond the fact that she brought you into the world, nurtured you, and continues to give you unconditional love—beyond simply *owing* her for all this—your bond is granted special moral status for its own sake, and should be the determining factor in deciding—despite her poor choice of profession. (I'm kidding. Not really…)

Virtue Ethics

So we've talked about only doing stuff we can universalize, treating persons with respect, maximizing net pleasure, and prioritizing the interests of loved ones. It's finally time to discuss a venerated ethical theory that focuses on the root of who we are—our character.

We're all familiar with the virtues of honesty, courage, humility, thrift and the like, as well as the vices of sloth, greed, gluttony, cowardice, and vanity. Virtue Ethicists argue that we should do our best to internalize and practice the former and avoid the latter—that ethics is all about developing good character. Why should we care about character? Because doing so will allow us to lead a good life.

This is the message ancient Greek philosopher Aristotle conveys to his son, Nicomachus, in the classic Nicomachean Ethics, transcribed from lectures given in Athens over two millennia ago. Cowardly, gluttonous, lazy people are usually dissatisfied with themselves. They're not leading good human lives—not living up to our amazing potential. They know it, everyone else knows it, and their experience as a person is simply less fulfilling than it could be.

On the other hand, brave, ambitious people who practice all things in moderation tend to be happier. They lead more satisfying existences more in line with what humans are capable of becoming. They push the boundaries of their potential, and as a result look back on their lives with a smile, rather than regret. *"If you want to live a good life,"* Virtue Ethicists say, *"then you should adhere to the time-tested virtues and avoid the time-tested vices."*

Do that, or simply ask yourself how a moral exemplar (or role model) would handle a given situation. For example, many Christian Virtue Ethicists model their lives after the life of Jesus, and when presented with any dilemma simply ask themselves, "What would Jesus do?" We might summarize the guidance of Virtue Ethics like this:

> ➢ *Follow the virtues, avoid the vices, and/or behave as would a moral exemplar.*

When it's unclear what your exemplar would do, and you're simply attempting to follow the virtues and avoid the vices, knowing which to apply and to what degree is a matter of good judgment. This is also true when virtues apparently recommend conflicting actions. Maybe being brave would require running into a burning building to search for survivors. But maybe being patient would require waiting for the fire department. When pressed to act, what's a thoughtful virtue ethicist to do?

These sorts of conflicts have led some to charge that Virtue Ethics is often imprecise— that it's more about the sort of person we ought to *be*, and less about what we morally ought to *do*. However, *wisdom*—considered by Socrates and Plato (who preceded and informed Aristotle) to be the most important virtue—allows a person to recognize the fine line between bravery and recklessness, thrift and miserliness, confidence and arrogance. It helps us discern when to be ambitious and when to be patient. And therefore the more of this key virtue we gain through study and experience, the easier time we have translating virtuous disposition into virtuous action.

Last, some have critiqued that the underling argument supporting Virtue Ethics seems selfish. "Ethics is about acting virtuously, and acting virtuously is important because it will enable us to live better lives, which will make us happier, more satisfied persons." This justifying argument isn't necessarily *bad*, but some have complained that its focus on personal benefit is a distinguishing feature of the theory, since the others provide other-regarding—or in the case of Kant, reason-regarding—reasons for their ultimate support.

However, our obligation to improve ourselves and lead good lives has also been presented as a civic duty. It was great-grandfather of Western philosophy, Socrates, who implored his fellow citizens to develop their characters not only for their own good, but for the good of Athenian society. As recounted in Plato's *Apology*, Socrates argues against the direct pursuit of material possessions in favor of moral goodness, for "wealth does not bring goodness, but goodness brings wealth and every other blessing, both to the individual and to the state."[1]

We've now briefly reviewed four ethical theories, each presenting a different account of the central requirements of moral behavior. While sometimes all four converge to recommend a similar action, often two or more will conflict—one mandating that you save the cancer researcher, another insisting that you save your mother (despite her profession).

So you may be wondering which you're supposed to follow. Enter Betsy Postow's "All-Things-Considered" approach to balancing conflicting moral obligations.

---

[1] Thanks to Dennis Dalton for help with this section, and for this passage from Plato's *Apology* from *The Last Days of Socrates* edited by Hugh Tredennick and Harold Tarrant, Penguin, 1993, 53-67.

Chapter 6

All Things Considered

Though some ethicists are what we might call exclusive Kantians, Utilitarians, Care Ethicists or Virtue Ethicists, the majority don't prioritize one theory to the detriment of the others. This is because all four seem to make good points, each expressing some ethical principle already consistent with common sense: Kantianism—we should be rationally consistent and treat persons with respect; Utilitarianism—we should promote good consequences (or more specifically, maximize net pleasure); Feminist Care Ethics—the interests of those close to us deserve special priority; Virtue Ethics—it's better to have good character than bad.

But while it may be clear that all four promote legitimate moral principles, it's often unclear which should guide our action when they conflict. As we saw with the kidnapping aliens example, Utilitarianism and Care Ethics sometimes produce incompatible recommendations. "If these demented aliens force me to choose, should I follow Utilitarianism and sacrifice my mom? Or Care Ethics and sacrifice the cancer researcher?"

One solution proposed by 20th century American philosopher Betsy Postow produces what she called an "All-Things-Considered" moral judgment. Postow argued that when presented with a moral dilemma we should identify which sorts of considerations are at play—respecting persons, promoting good consequences, honoring key relationships, developing good character, or some mix. This tells us which theories are most relevant in a particular case (maybe the interests of many rational agents are at stake, so Kantianism would have a lot to say) and which are less relevant (maybe the case deals with strangers only, so Care Ethics would have little to say).

Once we know which ethical theories are most and least relevant, deciding what to do is a matter of weighing and contrasting how powerfully the different theories would recommend different actions. That is, a strong Kantian consideration against an action would override a weak Utilitarian consideration for the same action, and vice versa.

For example, were I to see one of my students drowning in my neighbor's pond, I would have some obligation to respect my neighbor's property rights and not trespass on her lawn. This is a Kantian consideration that has some force. After all, fidelity to the concept of private property is necessary for a functioning economy, which produces necessary goods and services we might otherwise have to do without. Therefore, Kant would say since I can't universalize ignoring property boundaries, I ought not ignore them myself in this case. However, when we consider other morally relevant factors at play, the property claim in this

73

Kantian argument seems comparatively weak.

From the Utilitarian perspective, I assume drowning is a very unpleasurable experience, not to mention the negative impact my student's death would have on her friends and family. If I trespass on my neighbor's lawn just this one time her grass won't be damaged too terribly, and I suspect she'll actually thank me for the rescue, for it might prevent a lawsuit, as well as a devaluation of her property (homebuyers hate haunted ponds).

Further, though I may not know her very well, I have *some* relationship with all my students, and so long as saving her wouldn't detract from more pressing obligations to closer loved ones, that's a Care Ethics reason in favor of rescue.

Last, helping under these circumstances seems the sort of thing a caring, brave person would do, so Virtue Ethics would likely endorse rescuing her as well. If nothing else, the virtue of decisiveness would simply encourage me to spring into action as soon as possible.

And so we have a relatively weak Kantian prohibition on trespassing juxtaposed against a fairly strong Utilitarian argument in favor of rescuing, as well as additional weak support in favor of rescuing from both Feminist Care Ethics and Virtue Ethics. We might attempt to quantify the force of these recommendations on a -10 to +10 scale, similar to our Utilitarian calculus. -10 would correspond to the strongest possible prohibition, +10 the strongest possible obligation, and 0 would mean that particular theory doesn't seem to apply at all. Our calculations might look like this:

Rescue Drowning Student?

Kantianism: weak No (-2)

Utilitarianism: strong Yes (7)

Feminist Care Ethics: weak Yes (1)

Virtue Ethics: weak Yes (1)

Result: strong Yes (7)

It looks like I'd have an All-Things-Considered obligation to rescue the drowning student of a force of 7, which is pretty strong on our scale. Of course, things could get complicated. What if I'd have to dodge speeding traffic to save the student? I happen to live in the country, so evading a pack of rabid coyotes might be a more likely obstacle. Or what if when I arrive I find that *two* students are drowning rather than one, and I only have time and energy to save one? Or what if I find that instead of a student, the person drowning is a clone of Hitler!

These sorts of complex cases can and do happen. Well, nobody has to decide whether to save drowning Hitler clones... But morally relevant factors do sometimes pull in opposite directions, and the four dominant ethical theories do sometimes provide conflicting recommendations. However, Postow's approach gives us a way to work through these complexities to make decisions that are the best they can be, all things considered.

Last, notice that sometimes there's tension even *within* ethical theories. For example, adhering to the first formulation of Kant's Categorical Imperative (to only do stuff you could universalize) would put some emphasis on respecting property rights. But following the second formulation (to always treat persons with respect, and never as mere tools) would require considering the value and interests of the drowning student. After all, she possesses the capacity for higher reasoning Kant considers so important, and so while this wouldn't settle the matter alone, the point is simply that for Postow's approach to be effective, we should carefully consider cases from multiple angles— even from multiple angles within a single theory.

While the four dominant ethical theories and the All-Things-Considered approach to resolving conflicts among them can seem abstract and foreign at first, hopefully you can see how they're really just expansions on basic principles and strategies normal people already endorse and practice. Philosophers have done a great job carefully studying, evaluating, clarifying and in some cases improving common sense morality—of helping us to better understand our moral sense so we can apply it in a more consistent, accurate manner. But the basic elements were there all along, to be discovered and polished, not invented from scratch.

The final moral reasoning technique we'll explore is likely to seem similarly familiar. My bet is that you make and evaluate moral arguments by analogy all the time, even if you've never called them by that name.

Chapter 7

Argument by Analogy

Arguments by analogy use scenarios where the right thing to do is obvious to shed light on situations where the right thing to do is controversial. It's taken for granted that humans desire consistency in their judgments. And it's this shared commitment to treating like cases alike that gives arguments by analogy their persuasive and explanatory force.

Below are two famous examples (famous amongst ethicists, anyway), followed by tips on how to analyze this common moral reasoning technique. As you consider Singer and Jarvis-Thomson's paired scenarios, ask yourself whether they are relevantly similar, or whether key differences break down the connections the authors attempt to make.

SINGER'S DROWNING CHILD

Imagine you're walking down the street and see a small child drowning in a shallow pool. (What's up with all the drowning people?) No one else is around, and if you don't jump in and save them they'll surely drown. You happen to be wearing a new pair of expensive shoes, and if you jump in, they'll be ruined. However, it seems clear and uncontroversial that the child's life far outweighs the value of your shoes, and so most everyone would agree that the right thing to do is jump in and save them—new shoes be darned.

Well, philosopher Peter Singer argues that if you agree that we'd have a moral obligation to save the child in this scenario, you should also agree that we have a moral obligation to donate money to certain charities. Why? Thousands of children die every day from inexpensively treatable diseases such as diarrhea. Therefore, the next time we're in the market for a new pair of shoes, an iPod, an Xbox or whatever, we should instead donate that money to an organization like Oxfam who can use it to save the actual life of an actual child.

That's an argument by analogy. Singer says that if you agree with this moral assessment over here (a child's life is more important than new shoes when they're drowning in front of you), you should apply similar reasoning and reach a similar conclusion over there (a child's life is more important than new shoes when they're dying of an inexpensively treatable disease thousands of miles away).

Never mind that the urgency and vibrancy of a child drowning right in front of you would be more psychologically compelling and harder to ignore than a child dying of diarrhea on the other side of the planet. (Remember how psychology doesn't equal morality from chapter four?) The question is what we morally ought to do, not what we're psychologically apt to do, and given that these two cases seem relevantly similar, we ought to apply similar logic and reach similar conclusions. Or so says Singer.

JARVIS-THOMSON'S VIOLINIST

If you thought that was an odd argument, imagine that when you awake tomorrow morning you find yourself surrounded by a group of people in tuxedos and ballroom gowns. Looking to your left, you see that you're connected to one of them lying on a hospital bed via a series of medical tubes, with blood apparently flowing between you.

The leader notices that you're waking, stands and calmly says, "We are the Society of Music Lovers, and the gentleman to your left is a famous violinist—one of the world's greatest violinists, in fact. He has unfortunately been stricken by a harmful kidney disease, and your blood contains a rare protein which he needs constantly circulating through his veins to remain alive. You may find this situation inconvenient, but if you disconnect, he will surely die—thank you for your cooperation."

The question is, were you to awake to find yourself sharing your blood supply with a famous violinist, would have a moral obligation to remain connected? Doing so would require giving up most sports, and you'd likely find taking him to work and the grocery store a little awkward. But we're talking about the guy's life, so surely it would be unethical to (in effect) kill him just so you can keep up your hobbies and avoid awkwardness, right?

On the other hand, all you did was go to bed per usual. It's the Society of Music Lovers who hijacked your body and connected you in this way. Does the fact that the connection was made without your consent mean disconnecting would be less morally problematic? What if they said you only needed to remain connected for nine months—would that make a difference?

American philosopher Judith Jarvis-Thomson famously argued that you would have no obligation to remain connected for even one month, and that similar reasoning makes it clear that women who become pregnant as the result of rape have no obligation to maintain their pregnancy. Do you see the similarities between the cases?

In both the party providing life support did not consent to the connecting relationship. In both some third party brought the two together (the Society of Music Lovers in the first case and a rapist in the second). And in both the dependent party will die if the relationship is severed.

Therefore, if you conclude that you'd have no obligation to remain connected to the violinist, logical consistency demands that you conclude that rape victims have no obligation to maintain a resulting pregnancy. Or so says Jarvis-Thomson.

How to Analyze Arguments by Analogy

The best way to analyze an argument by analogy is to look for relevant differences between the cases being compared. For example, with Singer's drowning child/charitable giving argument, while we can know with certainty that the child will live if we jump in the water to save them, when we donate our shoe money to Oxfam we may wonder how much of it will actually purchase life-saving medicines. As it turns out, Oxfam is an exceptionally efficient charity. But can you think of other dissimilarities between the cases that might weaken the connection and undermine Singer's conclusion?

What about Jarvis-Thomson's violinist/abortion in cases of rape argument? One dissimilarity is that the famous violinist has presumably already lived a good portion of his life. We might therefore conclude that disconnecting and killing him (or simply allowing him to die if you prefer) wouldn't be quite as tragic as aborting an "Unborn Developing Human" or UDH (an intentionally neutral term I use when discussing the ethics of abortion) which has yet to experience the world at all. In other words, maybe we're OK with killing the violinist because he's old, which wouldn't apply to a UDH.

Or arguing in the other direction, the violinist presumably possesses the features of personhood we usually consider morally valuable—consciousness, the ability to feel pleasure and pain, the ability to engage in relationships, higher-order rationality—features that, depending on the stage of pregnancy, may not also be true of the UDH. And so if we think it would be morally permissible to disconnect from the violinist, it might be even easier to justify an abortion in cases of rape. In other words, if it's OK to disconnect from a violinist who possesses these key capacities, it would seem even more OK to disconnect from a UDH, which as of yet might not.

Of course, abortion is far too complex an issue to conclude anything definitive after a few short paragraphs. Just note that when evaluating an argument by analogy the goal is to look for *morally relevant* differences. That the Society of Music lovers hijacked your body while you were sleeping but most rapes occur while the victim is awake is a difference, but it doesn't seem to be a morally relevant difference. The morally relevant similarity is that the victim in both cases did not consent to the connection. Notice how this means that the violinist argument could not be used to justify the permissibility of abortions in cases where the pregnancy is the result of consensual sex. In defense of those sorts of abortions Jarvis-Thomson offers another creative argument by analogy involving "people seeds" which I consider in a YouTube lecture you're invited to watch.

So that's how we construct and evaluate arguments by analogy. To the extent that scenarios are relevantly similar, we should apply similar moral reasoning to them. Arguments by analogy are useful because they can shed light on tricky situations by referencing similar scenarios where we're more confident in our views. And they're powerful because we're implicitly committed to the values of fairness and consistency—of treating like cases alike.

But what's the basis for all this moral reasoning in the first place? If all we have are abstract theories to reference and similar cases to compare, even if we can neatly reconcile apparent conflicts with Postow's All-Things-Considered approach, how do we know we're not working with faulty assumptions? That we're not developing an intricate system that happens to be completely incorrect?

Though we can't rely on naked feeling, our moral sense, or intuition, provides such necessary input. And in combination with reason—and especially when we combine our reason with others—we can be reassured that our considered judgments move our views closer to what would seem to be most consistent with objective right and wrong. This approach certainly isn't infallible. But it may be the best we can do. How does it work?

Chapter 8

Intuition, Reflection &

Coherence

As you're finding, philosophers are a cerebral bunch. We're comfortable immersed in complex argumentation, demand precise reasoning, enjoy outlandish thought experiments, and relish complex *what ifs*.

My fellow *Star Trek* fans might be inclined to associate philosophers with the highly logical Vulcans. Both warn against following feelings or emotion, because bias and overreaction can cloud an otherwise clear mind.

But as you'll see, being attuned to our emotional side is actually quite necessary for moral philosophers. It's therefore more appropriate to associate ethicists with the half-Vulcan, half-human Spock, which suits me just fine, given Spock's super awesomeness…

THE VALUE OF MORAL INTUITION

Most philosophical ethicists agree that when it comes to our baseline, fundamental, no doubt moral convictions, like *slavery is wrong*, *killing innocents is usually wrong*, and *torture is usually wrong*, we shouldn't allow an elaborate theory to sway our certainty. If an ethical theory tells us slavery is permissible, that's reason to reject or revise the theory, or at least admit its limitations—not reason to endorse slavery.

Remember the "positive argument" from chapter three for why ethics isn't ice cream? I didn't use a sophisticated explanation to convince you moral subjectivism is fatally flawed. Rather, I exposed how endorsing subjectivism prevents us from criticizing baby torturers, and you could *directly see* the gravity of this weakness.

While philosophers are best known for using their minds, we actually need our hearts and minds to work together. We need our direct experience as creatures with moral sentiments to mesh with any theory we use to guide us when our moral vision might be less clear. Recall how Kantianism, Utilitarianism, Virtue Ethics and Feminist Care Ethics are all intimately tied to some moral axiom we take for granted as obviously true.

Upon reflection, we simply *know* or can directly see or feel that autonomy/respect, consequences/pleasure/pain, character and relationships are morally relevant concepts. This seems to be ingrained in our experience as persons, regardless of where or when we are—something that we're able to draw upon via a sense that some call intuition.

Our moral intuition is not a hindrance or even a luxury, but a critical necessity. We need an initial input to get all this theorizing off the ground. That doesn't mean we blindly defer to our gut feeling. Rather, consulting our moral sense is an integral part of careful moral reflection.

MORAL REFLECTION AND COHERENCE

One goal of philosophical ethics is to develop a rationally consistent set of moral beliefs that can be supported with sound argumentation. Why? Because *we should treat like cases alike* seems to be one of those baseline, fundamental principles that we can directly experience as true, and because we can't know for sure that our views pass this test until we've subjected them to evaluation and developed sound argumentation to support them.

At the same time, we want (and need) our gut-level moral judgments to inform our views. So we test them against similar cases, and put them in conversation with candidate ethical principles in an ongoing process of articulation, examination, reevaluation and revision.

We don't use ethical theories to *rationalize our prejudices* but rather to *improve our views*. And we come out on the other side of this process with a more consistent, coherent, set of moral beliefs.

One method for doing this was promoted by 20th century American political philosopher John Rawls, the goal of which is to obtain a state of "reflective equilibrium."

Maybe a person starts out convinced that homosexuality, abortion, and promiscuous sex are all three definitely and in all cases morally wrong. Then one day a friend suggests that it's inconsistent to hold those three views simultaneously, that there's some conflict of underlying principles or implications they're not appreciating. Shaken, the person asks themselves, are these views compatible?

In deciding, they search for an abstract principle that can organize and make sense of all three judgments. Rawls would advise that they go back and forth between candidate principles and their "considered convictions" (moral judgements in which they're currently most confident) attempting to achieve some degree of harmony. Ultimately they should be able to render all of their moral convictions logically consistent, but beginning with those that are most interesting or compelling is an excellent strategy.

Maybe there's a good way to reconcile and logically defend a simultaneous prohibition on homosexuality, abortion and promiscuous sex. Maybe there's not. (What do you think?) The point is that as a person goes back and forth between their convictions, searching for and testing different guiding principles, they may find that their baseline judgments aren't so certain after all. Maybe after discussion and reflection they conclude that homosexuality or some forms of abortion or promiscuous sex aren't as obviously immoral as they once seemed. Or maybe upon even further reflection they conclude that all three are even *more* immoral than they originally thought, as well as consistent with the exact same moral principle.

Whatever the case, coherence is a main aim, for anyone who fails to achieve it is subject to criticism on grounds that they're simply being illogical—a grave sin in the eyes of philosophers, scientists, and Vulcans. Remember, though, that like Spock, we must remain humble. Achieving reflective equilibrium, where our views are consistent with one another, as well as supportable with some rational explanation, doesn't mean they are forever set. Ethicist David DeGrazia articulates this attitude well.

> One must always be open to the possibility that our ethical convictions will require modification in light of further considerations. Thus, while we strive for a state of equilibrium in our total set of ethical convictions...we are never finished with moral inquiry. New problems arise. Fresh information and novel insights make us question old judgments. Moral reasoning is viewed as dynamic and is not expected to produce a final, rationally necessary theory.[2]

[2] *Taking Animals Seriously: Mental Life and Moral Status.* Cambridge University Press, 1996, 14.

You might be reluctant to accept DeGrazia's invitation to engage in periodic moral reflection, remaining open to new information that might give you reason to change your views.

If so, that's natural—the philosopher's pursuit of moral truth is an acquired attitude. But sometimes making yourself vulnerable is the only way to grow. What you stand to lose in comfort and certainty, you stand to gain in wisdom.

Chapter 9

Conclusion

So that's ethics in a nutshell. Philosophers use their capacity for higher reason to answer moral questions rather than blindly following their feelings, the crowd, or tradition. They construct arguments, share them with others, and think together in good faith (meaning honestly, with an open mind, having released their egos from whatever positions they currently happen to hold) in a cooperative pursuit of moral progress.

Some ethicists mentally segregate their religious and areligious moral reasoning. But many find ways for the two to work together in a complementary fashion.

Ethicists typically use the words "ought" and "should" in a prescriptive, rather than predictive, way. There's a difference between what people are psychologically likely to do, and what they morally ought to do, and philosophers are primarily interested in the latter. And while good law tracks morality, morality and legality are separable, distinct concepts, with the law serving as a shaky foundation for moral judgments.

Four theories dominate contemporary philosophical ethics: Kantianism, Utilitarianism, Feminist Care Ethics and Virtue Ethics, each of which is grounded in a morally relevant consideration most everyone takes for granted: respect for persons and logical consistency, outcomes and pleasure vs. pain, relationships and character. When it comes to applying those theories and making concrete judgments in real cases, one strategy is to consider what each would have us do separately, and then choose the option that enjoys the most "All-Things-Considered" support.

Argument by analogy is a common and powerful moral reasoning technique that resonates with our implicit commitment to treating like cases alike. And as we just saw, our intuitions play an important, foundational role in helping us decide which ethical theories and arguments are worthy of endorsement.

That's more than enough reading about philosophical ethics. It's time you started *doing* philosophical ethics with others, for philosophy, at its best, is a full contact sport.

As Harvard Professor Michael Sandel (whose book *Justice: What's the Right Thing to Do?* I can't recommend highly enough) says, "moral reflection is not a solitary pursuit but a public endeavor. It requires an interlocutor—a friend, a neighbor, a comrade, a fellow citizen. Sometimes the interlocutor can be imagined rather than real, as when we argue with ourselves. But we cannot discover the meaning of justice or the best way to live through introspection alone."[3]

Hopefully that red pill hasn't proven too bitter, and you haven't uncovered anything

3 Farrar, Straus and Giroux, 2009, 28.

nearly as disturbing as did Neo. Whatever the case, be honest in your analyses, humble in your conclusions, and find time to watch a little *Star Trek*. And remember that humility and courage are both prerequisites for and consequences of developing a more mature understanding of right and wrong. Kudos on beginning that journey.

If you enjoyed *Ethics in a Nutshell*, tell a friend and consider writing a brief review on Amazon.

Notaed Press is a small, independent publisher, and the success of our titles depends largely on the enthusiasm and goodwill of our readers.

So thanks for reading!

FURTHER READING

<u>Michael Sandel's *Justice: What's the Right Thing to Do?*</u>

Including engaging and accessible chapters on ethics (Utilitarianism, Kantianism) and political philosophy (Libertarianism, Liberalism, Communitarianism), and covering an impressive range of contemporary moral issues (military service, surrogate mothering, Affirmative Action, reparations), I've taught ethics using Harvard professor Michael Sandel's *Justice* for several years, and highly recommend it. Accompanying video lectures from Sandel himself are available at HarvardJustice.org, and video commentaries on most of the chapters from yours truly are available on my YouTube channel. As you'll find in my lecture on his 10th chapter, I actually disagree with one of Sandel's ultimate conclusions (spoiler—I am not a Communitarian). But it's still a fantastic book!

<u>The Stanford Encyclopedia of Philosophy Online</u>

Use the search function at Plato.Stanford.edu for concise articles on most anything philosophy, including the four dominant ethical theories (one at a time), subjectivism, reflective equilibrium, and much more.

<u>Mike Martin's *Everyday Morality*</u>

Includes coverage of "rights" theory, which I did not include here, but many smart people endorse. Plus, Professor Mike is an ethics bowl fan and volunteer judge, so his book has to be good.

<u>Hugh LaFollette's *Ethics in Practice*</u>

A superb applied ethics anthology featuring a nice balance of articles on issues including euthanasia, non-human animals, abortion, free speech, the death penalty, economic justice and the environment.

LECTURE NOTES

It's a good study habit to articulate and organize key concepts in a way that's consistent with your natural voice. To get you started, here's a rough outline of *Ethics in a Nutshell* that I might use as a first draft for lecture notes.

For brief lectures on each of the *Nutshell* chapters, visit YouTube.com/MattDeatonPhD.

And if you're serious about understanding and remembering this stuff, create your own notes. Highlighting or transposing the way I've explained it won't stick nearly as well as would the same concepts in your own words, true to your unique learning and comprehension style.

Chapter 1: Introduction

- **<u>The Philosopher's Basic Building Blocks:</u>** arguments (which are composed of premises intended to logically support conclusions)

- **<u>The Philosopher's Basic Disposition:</u>** devoted to the rational pursuit of truth, but simultaneously humble, and willing in principle to alter views if given good reason to do so

Chapter 2: What's "Ethics"?

- **<u>Philosophy:</u>** the reason-based attempt to answer life's big non-empirical questions

- **<u>Philosophical Ethics:</u>** the reason-based attempt to answer moral questions about what we ought to do

- **<u>Philosophy and Religion:</u>** can be complementary, and being able to reason from a philosophical perspective can enable interfaith dialogue, as well as show respect to fellow citizens in a multicultural society

Chapter 3: Why Ethics Isn't Ice Cream

- **Negative Argument**: just because people disagree over moral issues and there's no conclusive way to prove who's correct does not mean ethics is subjective, or a matter of personal taste

    - Why? Consider how equally intelligent people disagree over whether intelligent life exists beyond Earth, and how we can't conclusively prove who's correct—doesn't mean aliens' existence is a matter of personal taste (they exist or don't independent of our beliefs, just like the shape of Earth is independent of our beliefs).

- **Positive Argument**: moral subjectivism (or the view that ethics is a matter of personal opinion) has repugnant, unacceptable implications, and should therefore be rejected

- ○ What sort of repugnant, unacceptable implications? Like having to say that a guy who believes torturing babies for pleasure is morally permissible is correct. Or that a person who kidnaps and tortures us can't be criticized on moral grounds.

Chapter 4: Three Key Distinctions

- **Prescriptive vs. Predictive**

  - ○ When ethicists use the terms "should" or "ought" they're usually using them in the morally prescriptive sense, not the future predictive sense.

- **Morality vs. Psychology**

  - ○ Deciding what a person morally ought to do shouldn't be conflated with what a person would be psychologically prone or likely to do.

- **Morality vs. Legality**

  - We can't consult the law when answering moral questions, for legal doesn't necessarily = moral and illegal doesn't necessarily = immoral. How do we know this? Consider current or past laws that are or were obviously unethical (such as those legitimizing the sale of human beings, or those forbidding women the right to vote).

Chapter 5: The Four Dominant Ethical Theories

- **I: Kantianism**

  - *Only do stuff we could rationally will everyone else do, too*

  - *Treat persons with respect (never as mere tools)*

- Supporting argument: If we value anything, we should value reason itself, because it facilitates valuations in the first place; respecting fellow persons, who also possess the capacity for higher reason, is matter of logical consistency (since we're no more special than they are given our roughly equal reasoning abilities).

- **II: Utilitarianism**

  - *Maximize net pleasure*

    - How? Examine options, calculate net pleasure of each, and do whichever maximizes net pleasure for all.

      - Supporting argument: Pleasure the only thing

intrinsically
valuable; all
creatures'
pleasure/pain
equally important.

- **III: Feminist Care Ethics**

  - *Honor obligations arising from relational ties and prioritize the interests of loved ones*

  - Loved ones matter for their own sake, not because consequences would be bettered or reason appeased.

    - Supporting argument: Humans are fundamentally interdependent creatures; the importance of relational ties is an undeniable feature of ethical decision-making.

- **IV: Virtue Ethics**

  - *Practice the acknowledged virtues and avoid the acknowledged vices*

    - Honesty, courage, humility, thrift, temperance; sloth, greed, gluttony, vanity

  - *Or follow a role model or moral exemplar*

    - <u>Supporting argument</u>: Building a virtuous character will likely lead to a fulfilling life.

Chapter 6: All Things Considered

- **<u>Need to Balance</u>**: conflicting recommendations from ethical theories

  - Could choose one, always follow, but all four seem compelling.

- **<u>Postow's Solution</u>**: weigh the force of each recommendation within its own realm against the force of the other recommendations within their realms; go with whichever option enjoys the most overall support

- We intuitively make rough balancing judgments like this already. Postow's "All-Things-Considered" approach simply formalizes this natural practice.

Chapter 7: Argument by Analogy

- **Basic Structure**: two cases are relevantly similar; therefore we should judge them consistently (apply reasoning from clear-cut case to tougher, less clear, relevantly similar cases)

- **How to Analyze**: look for morally relevant differences between the scenarios

  - If there are none, the reasoning holds—should apply similar moral logic to both.

o   If there are some, we may have
      reason to treat the cases
      differently.

Chapter 8: Intuition, Reflection & Coherence

- **Value of Moral Intuitions**: our bedrock
  moral convictions serve as necessary
  input into the moral reasoning process

- **Reflection and Coherence**: achieving
  consistency among our views via
  reflection enables the identification of
  overarching principles that can be
  applied to new areas

Chapter 9: Conclusion

- Recap of the book
- Encouragement to reason in good faith
  with fellow citizens
- Reminder to watch a little *Star Trek*

For lectures on the chapters, sample reflection/exam questions, and to join the conversation visit

EthicsinaNutshell.org

To connect with Dr. Deaton visit

MattDeaton.com

And if you enjoyed this introduction to the philosopher's approach to morality, take an (or another) ethics class, support your local ethics bowl (NHSEB.unc.edu/regionals), and check out additional ethics and political philosophy lecture videos at

YouTube.com/MattDeatonPhD

Rosalind Hursthouse and Edward Langerak on Abortion
Matt Deaton
3 months ago
Brief lecture on Husthouse's "Virtue Theory and Abortion" and Edward Langerak's "Abortion: Listening to the Middle," featuring...

Sandel's Justice Chapter 10: Justice and the Common Good
Matt Deaton
3 years ago
Sandel's view on "public reason" and why it is incorrect.

Sandel's Justice Chapter 6: Rawls
Matt Deaton
3 years ago
The political philosophy of John Rawls simplified with stuffed animals and Halloween candy.

Noonan and Thomson on Abortion
Matt Deaton
4 months ago
Brief lecture on John T. Noonan and Judith Jarvis-Thomson's classic abortion ethics articles.